ISH THE FISH

WRITTEN BY LINDA H. MILLER
ILLUSTRATED BY PAMELA S. TITTLE

ISH THE FISH

Written by Linda H. Miller
Illustrated by Pamela S. Tittle

Copyright 2019 by Linda H. Miller
All rights reserved. No part of this book may be reproduced,
stored in a retrieval system or transmitted in any form,
or by any means, electronic, mechanical, photocopying, recording,
or otherwise, without the prior permission of the author.

Printed in the United States of America

Library of Congress Number: 2019938270
International Standard Book Number: 978-1-60126-624-8

Published by
Masthof Press
219 Mill Road
Morgantown, PA 19543
www.Masthof.com

ISH THE FISH

On her first birthday

Grandpa gave Sofia

a blue beta

that she called Ish.

Sofia peers into the aquarium and watches the fish.

"Guppies," says Grammy.

"Ish," says Sofia.

Sofia peeks over the counter

and watches the fish.

"Beta," says Grandpa.

"Ish," says Sofia.

Sofia pauses at the garden pond

and watches the fish.

"Koi," says cousin Liv.

"Ish," says Sofia.

Sofia lingers at the aquarium window

and watches the fish.

"Clownfish," says Mommy.

"Ish," says Sofia.

Sofia leans over the rail of the touch pool

and watches the fish.

"Stingray," says Aunt Aimee.

"Ish," says Sofia.

Sofia crouches on the step by the big tank

and watches the fish.

"Shark," says Daddy.

"Ish," says Sofia and her eyes get big.

Sofia settles in her highchair
and watches the fish.
"Ish," says Grammy.

"Yum," says Sofia
and she eats them all.

THE END